Presented to :

Marianne Chamberlain
Worthy Matron
1987

From :

Wayne & Pauline Lohr
Worthy Patron - Prompter

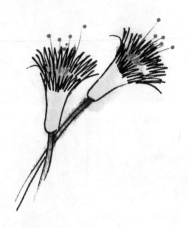

By Helen Steiner Rice

Loving
Thoughts
Helen
Steiner Rice

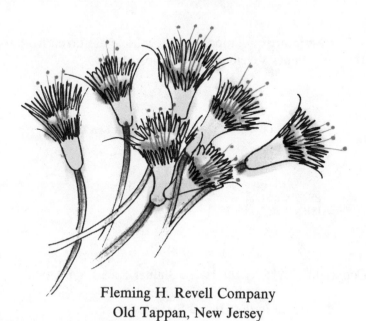

Fleming H. Revell Company
Old Tappan, New Jersey

Book Design and Illustrations by
John Okladek

The Scripture quotations in this volume are taken from the King James Version of the Bible.

Library of Congress Cataloging in Publication Data

Rice, Helen Steiner.
  Loving thoughts.

  1. Christian poetry, American. I. Title.
PS3568.I28L59   1985   811'.54   84-13413
ISBN 0-8007-1311-7

Contents

Part 2   Faith   **49**

Part 3   Special Days   85

★ *Newly published in book format.*

Publisher's Foreword

It was not without a little fear and apprehension that I accepted the assignment in Cincinnati. As a former journalist, I'd always enjoyed the dialogue—and the rapport—that develops between two people in a successful interview. Two-sided, give-and-take. Questions well chosen, well parried, and sometimes yielding provocative insight into a secret heart, a private life.

This was different. There would be no respondent to my queries. . . . Helen Steiner Rice had gone to her great reward on April 23, 1981, just twenty-six days shy of her eighty-first birthday.

And now, a little more than two years later, as managing editor I'd gone to research the files she had left behind, to unearth new materials that might lend themselves to publication.

Prior to this, my association with her had been rather remote. I'd written one piece for her, another about her, and granted hundreds of requests to quote her poems. She was revered by her readers 'round the world, and many thought they knew her. I imagined I did.

But this was different. It called for peering into, even scrutinizing, the effects of the woman once described as "the poet laureate of popular verse"—without her by my side. To begin was an awesome task; to complete it became a chastening one.

Seventeen weathered and dusty cartons rested in mute testimony. There were bits and pieces salvaged from her early dreams when she was Helen Elaine Steiner: old newspaper and magazine articles chronicling her rise as a speechmaker, motivator, saleswoman; gold-framed citations; little gifts that bespoke tender sentiment; her beginning efforts as a poet, and a few of her final ones, some completed, some left suspended on the page.

And there were the letters. Hundreds of them. She meticulously kept copies of her correspondence to friends, fans, fellow employees. They—as she had penned her poems—were written to celebrate, to honor, to commemorate, to counsel and console. Many were written in rhyme.

What emerged in this one-sided interview was the spirit of a woman who always exercised great personal concern for humanity, but who rarely exposed her own humanness, her own vulnerability. I became increasingly aware of her private, haunting thoughts on career, health, death, marriage. She was publicly optimistic, privately lonely, and though she was not known for it, much of her writing was peppered with humor. Always there was the consistent, insistent, persistent deference to the God she believed guided her pen and her life. It was never her talent, only His.

* * * * *

The material ultimately fell into several categories, some still being refined: the correspondence mentioned earlier, biographical data, and the poems, finished and unfinished.

For this initial venture, *Loving Thoughts,* we decided to respond to the demand of her legion of admirers for more of her poems. We chose twenty-eight works that had never appeared in book format. They were originally created by Mrs. Rice during her long association with the Gibson Greeting Card Company. Augmenting them are sixty-seven rarely used pieces that have been culled from our previous publications. Each was selected with infinite care, and each lends itself to the total theme.

In any interview there needs to be a summation. What better than one from the poet herself:

> There is no night without dawning,
> No Winter without Spring,
> And beyond death's dark horizon
> Our hearts will once more sing—

Helen Steiner Rice's thoughts and words evoke love whether read or spoken or sung.

NORMA F. CHIMENTO
Managing Editor

Loving Thoughts

Part 1

Dear Friends

"Dear Friends"

We all need words to live by,
To inspire us and guide us,
Words to give us courage
When the trials of life betide us—
And the words that never fail us
Are the words of God above,
Words of comfort and of courage
Filled with wisdom and with love—
They are ageless and enduring
They have lived through generations,
There's no question left unanswered
In Our Father's revelations—
And in this ever-changing world
God's words remain unchanged,
For though through countless ages
They've been often rearranged,
The *truth* shines through all changes
Just as *bright today* as when
Our Father made the *Universe*
And breathed His Life in men—
And the words of inspiration
That I write for you today
Are just the old enduring truths
Said in a rhythmic way—
And if my "borrowed words of truth"
In some way touch your heart,
Then I am deeply thankful
To have had a little part
In sharing these *God-given lines,*
And I hope you'll share them, too,
With family, friends, and loved ones
And all those dear to you.

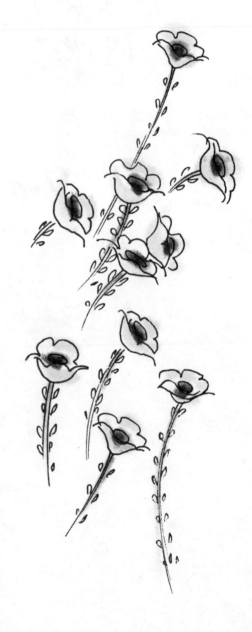

Fill Your Heart
With Thanksgiving

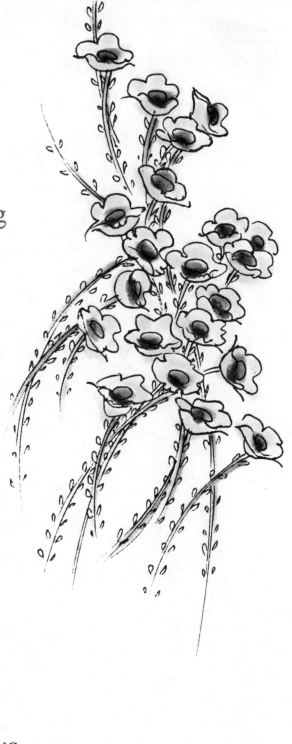

Take nothing for granted,
  for whenever you do
The "joy of enjoying"
  is lessened for you—
For we rob our own lives
  much more than we know
When we fail to respond
  or in any way show
Our thanks for the blessings
  that daily are ours . . .
The warmth of the sun,
  the fragrance of flowers,
The beauty of twilight,
  the freshness of dawn,
The coolness of dew
  on a green velvet lawn,
The kind little deeds
  so thoughtfully done,
The favors of friends
  and the love that someone
Unselfishly gives us
  in a myriad of ways,
Expecting no payment
  and no words of praise—
Oh, great is our loss
  when we no longer find
A thankful response
  to things of this kind,
For the JOY of ENJOYING
  and the FULLNESS of LIVING
Are found in the heart
  that is filled with THANKSGIVING.

In Times Like These

We read the headlines daily
  and listen to the news,
We shake our heads despairingly
  and glumly sing the blues—
We are restless and dissatisfied
  and we do not feel secure,
We are vaguely discontented
  with the things we must endure . . .
This violent age we live in
  is filled with nameless fears
As we listen to the newscasts
  that come daily to our ears,
And we view the threatening future
  with sad sobriety
As we're surrounded daily
  by increased anxiety . . .
How can we find security
  or stand on solid ground
When there's violence and dissension
  and confusion all around;
Where can we go for refuge
  from the rising tides of hate,
Where can we find a haven
  to escape this shameful fate . . .

So instead of reading headlines
    that disturb the heart and mind,
Let us open up the BIBLE
    and in doing so we'll find
That this age is no different
    from the millions gone before,
But in every hour of crisis
    God has opened up a door
For all who seek His guidance
    and trust His all-wise plan,
For God provides protection
    beyond that devised by man . . .
And we learn that each TOMORROW
    is not ours to understand,
But lies safely in the keeping
    of the great Creator's Hand,
And to have the steadfast knowledge
    that WE NEVER WALK ALONE
And to rest in the assurance
    that our EVERY NEED IS KNOWN
Will help dispel our worries,
    our anxieties and care,
For doubt and fear are vanquished
    in THE PEACEFULNESS OF PRAYER.

God Gave Man the Earth to Enjoy—
Not to Destroy

"The earth is the Lord's and the fullness thereof"—
He gave it to man as a Gift of His Love
So all men might live as He hoped that they would,
Sharing together all things that were good . . .
But man only destroyed "the good earth of God"—
He polluted the air and ravished the sod,
He cut down the forests with ruthless disdain,
And the earth's natural beauty he perverted for gain . . .
And all that God made and all that He meant
To bring man great blessings and a life of content
Have only made man a "giant of greed"
In a world where the password is "SEX, SIN and SPEED" . . .
And now in an age filled with violent dissent
Man finds he's imprisoned in his own discontent—
He has taken the earth that God placed in man's care
And built his own "hell" without being aware
That the future we face was fashioned by man
Who in ignorance resisted GOD'S BEAUTIFUL PLAN,
And what God created to be paradise
Became by man's lust and perversion and vice
A "caldron of chaos" in a "fog of pollution"
To which man can find no cure or solution—
How far man will go to complete his destruction
Is beyond a computer's robot deduction.

**The earth is the Lord's, and the fulness thereof;
the world, and they that dwell therein.**

Psalms 24:1

In Reverent Reverie
God Came to Me

I sat among the people
   in the church of my childhood and youth . . .
I came back to sing the songs of praise
   and to hear "the words of truth" . . .
I looked into the faces
   of the young folks and the old . . .
And listened, as I used to,
   to "THE SWEETEST STORY EVER TOLD" . . .
I had come back home to visit
   and to meet friends in glad reunion . . .
But the Sunday that I went to church
   turned out to be "COMMUNION" . . .
And so it was, when I arose
   from my "COMMUNION PRAYER" . . .
I no longer saw JUST FACES,
   for GOD was standing there.

Meet Life's Trials With Smiles

There are times when life overwhelms us
And our trials seem too many to bear,
It is then we should stop to remember
God is standing by ready to share
The uncertain hours that confront us
And fill us with fear and despair
For God in His goodness has promised
That the cross He gives us to wear
Will never exceed our endurance
Or be more than our strength can bear . . .
And secure in that blessed assurance
We can smile as we face tomorrow
For God holds the key to the future
And no sorrow or care need we borrow!

. . . for the Lord preserveth the faithful . . .

Psalms 31:23

Tomorrow
I'll Think About God

Not today when I am busy,
Not today when there's so much to do,
Not today while I'm young and eager
And life is far-reaching and new—
But tomorrow when I am older
And the tempo of life is less,
I'll have more time for praying
And for meditating, I guess . . .
But time is swift in its passing
And before we are really aware
We find ourselves growing older
And daily in need of GOD'S care . . .
And while GOD is always ready
To help us and lead us along,
Because we have tarried and wasted
Our young days in "dancing and song,"
We find we are not well acquainted
With the wonderful love of THE LORD
And we feel very strange in HIS PRESENCE
And unworthy of OUR FATHER' REWARD—
For only the children who seek HIM
With hearts yet untouched and still clean
Can ever experience HIS GREATNESS
And know what HIS LOVE can mean . . .
So waste not the hours of "LIFE'S MORNING,"
Get acquainted with GOD when you're born,
And when you come to "LIFE'S EVENING,"
It will shine like "THE GLORY of MORN"!

If You Haven't Succeeded, Maybe "New Management" Is Needed!

Nothing goes right,
  everything's wrong,
You stumble and fall
  as you trudge along,
The other guy wins,
  but you always lose,
Whatever you hear
  is always "bad news" . . .
Well, here's some advice
  that's worth a try,
Businessmen use it
  when they want a "NEW HIGH"—
So "old management" goes
  and the "new" comes in,
For this is the way
  "BIG BUSINESS" CAN WIN . . .

So if you are trying
    to manage your life,
Yet all around
    is chaos and strife,
Make up your mind
    that you, too, need a change
And start making plans
    to somehow rearrange
The way that you think
    and the things that you do
And what are the things
    that are hindering you . . .
Then put yourself under
    GOD'S "MANAGEMENT" now,
And when HE takes over
    you'll find that somehow
Everything changes,
    "OLD THINGS PASS AWAY,"
And "the darkness of night"
    becomes "the brightness of day"—
For GOD can transform
    and change into "WINNERS"
The LOSERS and SKEPTICS
    and even the SINNERS!

Your Life Will Be Blest If You Look for the Best

It's easy to grow downhearted
   when nothing goes your way,
It's easy to be discouraged
   when you have a troublesome day,
But trouble is only a challenge
   to spur you on to achieve
The BEST that God has to offer
   if you have the FAITH to BELIEVE!

Listen in Silence
If You Would Hear

Silently the green leaves grow
In silence falls the soft, white snow
Silently the flowers bloom
In silence sunshine fills a room
Silently bright stars appear
In silence velvet night draws near ...
And silently GOD enters in
To free a troubled heart from sin
For GOD works silently in lives
For nothing spiritual survives
Amid the din of a noisy street
Where raucous crowds with hurrying feet
And "blinded eyes" and "deafened ear"
Are never privileged to hear
The message GOD wants to impart
To every troubled, weary heart
For only in a QUIET PLACE
Can man behold GOD FACE to FACE!

Be still, and know that I am God.

Psalms 46:10

In His Footsteps

When someone does a
     kindness
   It always seems to me
That's the way God up in
     heaven
   Would like us all to be . . .
For when we bring some
     pleasure
   To another human heart,
We have followed in His
     footsteps
   And we've had a little part
In serving Him who loves us—
   For I am very sure it's true
That in serving those
     around us
We serve and please Him,
     too.

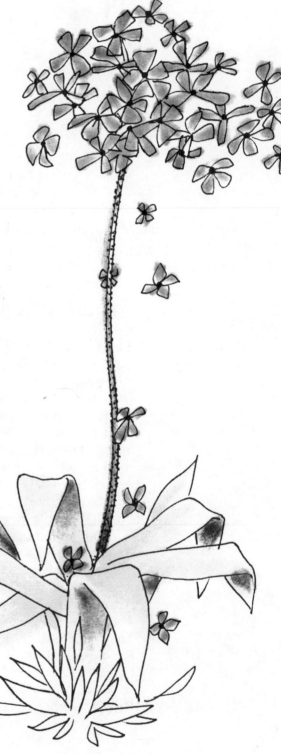

For You a Prayer
That God Will Keep
You in His Care

Prayers for big and little things
Fly heavenward on "angels' wings"—
And He who walked by the Galilee
And touched the blind and made them see,
And cured the man who long was lame
When he but called God's holy name,
Will keep you safely in His care
And when you need Him He'll be "There"!

For the Lord shall be thy confidence . . .

Proverbs 3:26

The Legend of the Spider
and the Silken Strand
Held in God's Hand

There's an old Danish Legend
  with a lesson for us all
Of an ambitious spider
  and his rise and his fall,
Who wove his sheer web
  with intricate care
As it hung suspended
  somewhere in midair,
Then in soft, idle luxury
  he feasted each day
On the small, foolish insects
  he enticed as his prey,
Growing ever more arrogant
  and smug all the while
He lived like a "king"
  in self-satisfied style—
And gazing one day
  at the sheer strand suspended,
He said, "I don't need this,"

so he recklessly rended
The strand that had held
  his web in its place
And with sudden swiftness
  the web crumpled in space—
And that was the end
  of the spider who grew
So arrogantly proud
  that he no longer knew
That it was the strand
  that reached down from above
Like the chord of God's grace
  and His infinite love
That links our lives
  to the great unknown,
For man cannot live
  or exist on his own—
And this old legend
  with simplicity told
Is a moral as true
  as the legend is old—
Don't sever the "lifeline"
  that links you to
THE FATHER IN HEAVEN
  WHO CARES FOR YOU.

Each Day Brings
a Chance to Do Better

How often we wish for another chance
   to make a fresh beginning,
A chance to blot out our mistakes
   and change failure into winning—
And it does not take a special time
   to make a brand-new start,
It only takes the deep desire
   to try with all our heart
To live a little better
   and to always be forgiving
And to add a little "sunshine"
   to the world in which we're living—
So never give up in despair
   and think that you are through,
For there's always a tomorrow
   and a chance to start anew.

The Way to Love and Peace

There is no thinking person
Who can stand untouched today
And view the world around us
Slowly drifting to decay
Without feeling deep within them
A silent, unnamed dread
As they contemplate the future
That lies frighteningly ahead . . .
And as the "CLOUDS OF CHAOS"
Gather in man's muddled mind,
And he searches for the answer
He ALONE can never find,
Let us recognize we're facing
Problems man has never solved,
And with all our daily efforts
Life grows more and more involved,
But our future will seem brighter
And we'll meet with less resistance
If we call upon our Father
And seek Divine Assistance . . .
For the spirit can unravel
Many tangled, knotted threads
That defy the skill and power
Of the world's best hands and heads,
And our plans for growth and progress,
Of which we all have dreamed,
Cannot survive materially
Unless OUR SPIRITS are redeemed . . .
For only when the mind of man
Is united with the soul
Can LOVE and PEACE combine to make
Our lives complete and whole.

. . . the fruit of the Spirit is love . . . peace. . . .

Galatians 5:22

What Is Sin?

We ask "What Is Sin"
   and how does it begin,
Does it come from Without
   or begin from Within?
Well, sin is much more
   than an Act or a Deed,
More than "false witness"
   or avarice and greed,
More than adultery
   or killing and stealing,
Sin starts with a Thought
   or an unworthy feeling
Long before it becomes
   an Act, Word or Deed,
For it grows deep within
   like a poisonous weed—
It's something we nurture
   and then cultivate
By conjuring up evils
   we then imitate,
And the longer we dwell
   on this evil within
The greater our urge

and desire to sin,
And the less our restraint
of unwholesome sensations
To deny to our bodies
full gratifications—
And the more that we sin
the less we detect
That in sinning we lose
our own self-respect
And slowly we sink
to a still lower level
Until we become merely
"dupes of the devil,"
For sin is so subtle
and it slips in with ease
And it gets a firm hold
when we Do As We Please—
So ask God to help you
to conquer desire
Aroused by the thoughts
that have set you afire,
And remember in sinning
there is no lasting joy
For all sin can do
is Degrade and Destroy!

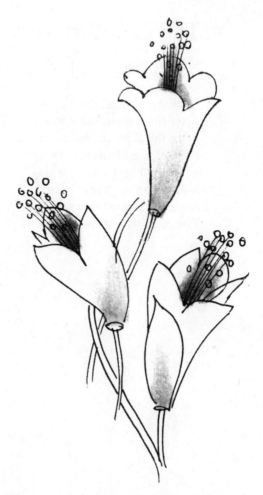

The Comfort and
Sweetness of Peace

After the clouds, the sunshine,
After the winter, the spring,
After the shower, the rainbow—
For life is a changeble thing;
After the night, the morning
Bidding all darkness cease,
After life's cares and sorrows,
The comfort and sweetness of peace.

Listen With Your Heart

Memories are a treasure
   time cannot take away . . .
So may you be surrounded
   by happy ones today . . .
May all the love and tenderness
   of golden years well spent
Come back today to fill your heart
   with beauty and content . . .
And may you walk down MEMORY LANE
   and meet the one you love
For while you cannot see him,
   he'll be watching from above . . .
And if you trust your dreaming
   your faith will make it true . . .
And if you listen with your heart
   he'll come and talk with you . . .
So for his sake be happy
   and show him that his love
Has proven strong and big enough
   to reach down from above . . .
And you will never walk alone
   when Memory's Door swings wide . . .
For you'll find that your beloved
   is always at your side.

**And this is the promise that he hath
promised us, even eternal life.**

1 John 2:25

To Really Live Is
to Give and Forgive!

Since GOD forgives us
    we, too, must forgive
And resolve to do better
    each day that we live
By constantly trying
    to be like HIM more nearly
And to trust in HIS wisdom
    and love HIM more dearly.

Take Time to Be Kind

Kindness is a virtue
   given by THE LORD,
It pays dividends in happiness
   and joy is its reward . . .
For, if you practice kindness
   in all you say and do,
THE LORD will wrap HIS kindness
   around your heart and you . . .
And wrapped within HIS kindness
   you are sheltered and secure
And under HIS direction
   your way is safe and sure.

Your Problems!
My Problems!
Our Problems!

Whatever your problem,
Whatever your cross,
Whatever your burden,
Whatever your loss,
You've got to believe me
You are not alone,
For all of the troubles
And trials you have known
Are faced at this minute
By others like you
Who also cry out,
"Oh, GOD, what shall I do?" . . .
I read many letters
From far countries and places,
I see eyes of sadness
In hundreds of faces,
And I, too, feel "the thorns
And the bruises of life"
And "the great stabbing pain
Of sorrow's sharp knife,"
But I know in my heart
This will, too, pass away . . .
And so as you read this
I implore you today
Find comfort in knowing
This is GOD'S way of saying
"COME UNTO ME"
And never cease praying,
For whatever your problem
Or whatever your sorrow
GOD holds "THE KEY"
To a BRIGHTER TOMORROW!

Rest in the Lord, and wait patiently for him.

Psalms 37:7

38

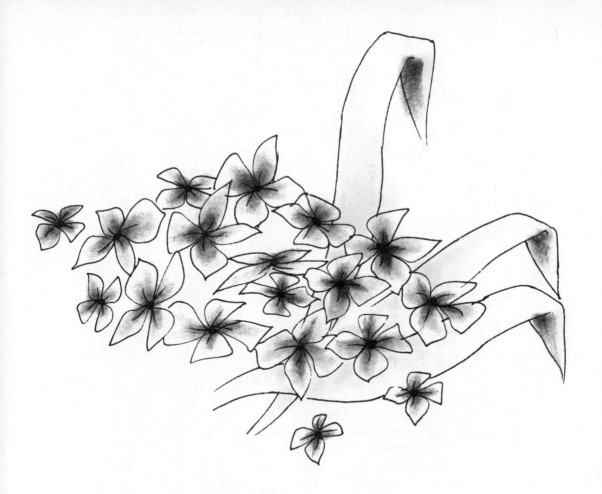

The World Needs
Friendly Folks
Like You

In this troubled world
  it's refreshing to find
Someone who still has
  the time to be kind,
Someone who still has
  the faith to believe
That the more you give
  the more you receive,
Someone who's ready
  by thought, word or deed
To reach out a hand
  in the hour of need.

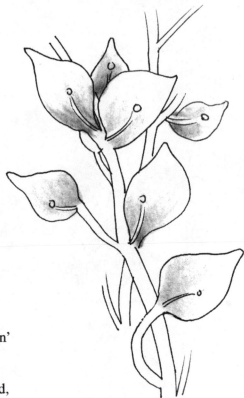

Stop Supposin'

Don't start your day by supposin'
  that trouble is just ahead,
It's better to stop supposin'
  and start with a prayer instead,
And make it a prayer of *Thanksgiving*
  for the wonderful things God has wrought
Like the beautiful sunrise and sunset,
  "God's Gifts" that are free
  and not bought—
For what is the use of supposin'
  the dire things that could happen to you
And worry about some misfortune
  that seldom if ever comes true—
But instead of just idle supposin'
  step forward to meet each new day
Secure in the knowledge God's near you
  to lead you each step of the way—
For supposin' the worst things will happen
  only helps to make them come true
And you darken the bright, happy moments
  that the dear Lord has given to you—
So if you desire to be happy
  and get rid of the *"misery of dread"*
Just give up *"Supposin' the worst things"*
  and look for *"the best things"* instead.

Wish Not for Ease or to Do as You Please!

If wishes worked like magic
And plans worked that way, too,
And if everything you wished for,
Whether Good or Bad for You,
Immediately were granted
With no effort on your part,
You'd experience no fulfillment
Of your spirit or your heart—
For things achieved too easily
Lose their charm and meaning, too,
For it is life's difficulties
And the trial-times we go through
That make us strong in spirit
And endow us with the will
To surmount the insurmountable
And to climb the highest hill—
So wish not for the Easy Way
To win your heart's desire,
For the joy's in overcoming
And withstanding "flood and fire"—
For to triumph over trouble
And grow stronger with defeat
Is to win the kind of victory
That will make your life complete.

A Special Prayer for You

Oh, Blessed Father, hear this prayer
   and keep all of us in Your care
Give us patience and inner sight, too,
   just as You often used to do
When on the shores of the Galilee
   You touched the blind and they could see
And cured the man who long was lame
   when he but called Your Holy Name!

You Are So Great . . .
   we are so small . . .
And when trouble comes
   as it does to us all
There's so little that we can do
   except to place our trust in You!

So take the Saviour's loving Hand
  and do not try to understand
Just let Him lead you where He will
  through "pastures green and waters still"
And place yourself in His loving care
  And He will gladly help you bear
Whatever lies ahead of you
  and God will see you safely through
And no earthly pain is ever too much
  if God bestows His merciful touch.

So I commend you into His care
  with a loving thought and a Special Prayer
And always remember, Whatever Betide You
  God is always beside you
And you cannot go beyond His love and care
  for we are all a part of God,
  and God is everywhere!

**. . . pray to thy Father which is in secret; and thy
Father which seeth in secret shall reward thee openly.**

Matthew 6:6

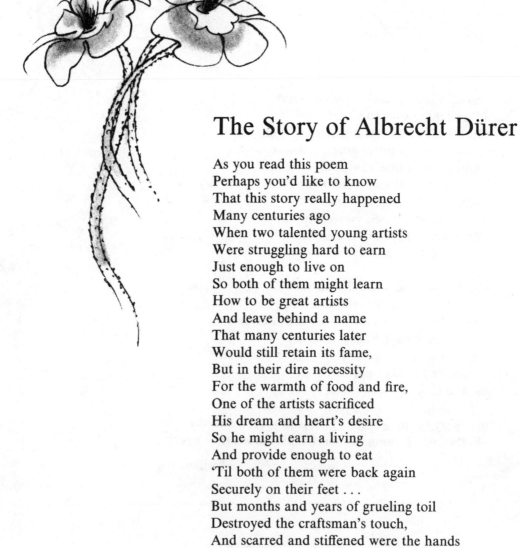

The Story of Albrecht Dürer

As you read this poem
Perhaps you'd like to know
That this story really happened
Many centuries ago
When two talented young artists
Were struggling hard to earn
Just enough to live on
So both of them might learn
How to be great artists
And leave behind a name
That many centuries later
Would still retain its fame,
But in their dire necessity
For the warmth of food and fire,
One of the artists sacrificed
His dream and heart's desire
So he might earn a living
And provide enough to eat
'Til both of them were back again
Securely on their feet . . .
But months and years of grueling toil
Destroyed the craftsman's touch,
And scarred and stiffened were the hands
That held promise of so much,
He could no longer hold a brush

The way he used to do,
And the dream he once had cherished,
No longer could come true . . .
So uncomplainingly he lived
With his friend who had succeeded
Who now could purchase all the things
They once had so much needed . . .
But the famous ALBRECHT DÜRER,
The friend we're speaking of,
Was always conscious that he owed
A debt of thanks and love
To one who sacrificed his skill
So that Dürer might succeed,
But how can anyone repay
A sacrificial deed,
But when he saw these hands in prayer
He decided he would paint
A picture for the world to see
Of this "unheralded saint" . . .
So down through countless ages
And in many, many lands
All men could see the beauty
In these toilworn PRAYING HANDS . . .
And seeing, they would recognize
That behind FAME and SUCCESS
Somebody sacrificed a dream
For another's happiness.

Storms Bring Out the Eagles
but the Little Birds Take Cover

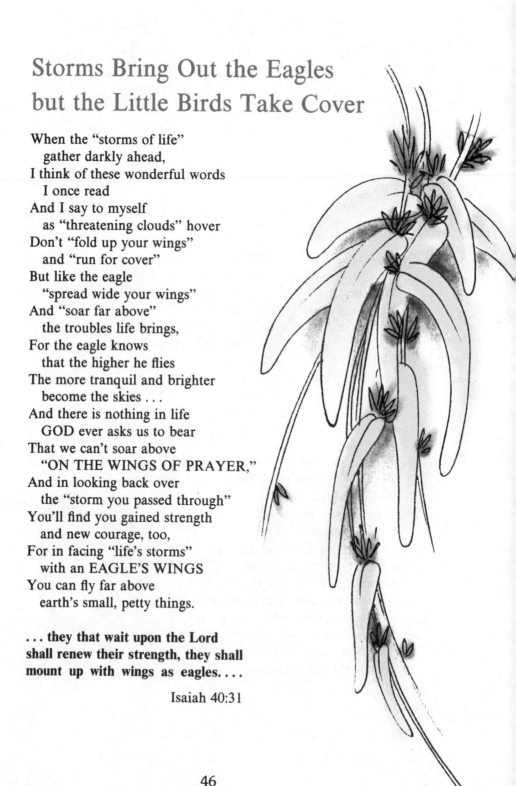

When the "storms of life"
   gather darkly ahead,
I think of these wonderful words
   I once read
And I say to myself
   as "threatening clouds" hover
Don't "fold up your wings"
   and "run for cover"
But like the eagle
   "spread wide your wings"
And "soar far above"
   the troubles life brings,
For the eagle knows
   that the higher he flies
The more tranquil and brighter
   become the skies . . .
And there is nothing in life
   GOD ever asks us to bear
That we can't soar above
   "ON THE WINGS OF PRAYER,"
And in looking back over
   the "storm you passed through"
You'll find you gained strength
   and new courage, too,
For in facing "life's storms"
   with an EAGLE'S WINGS
You can fly far above
   earth's small, petty things.

**. . . they that wait upon the Lord
shall renew their strength, they shall
mount up with wings as eagles. . . .**

Isaiah 40:31

46

God Bless You and
Keep You in His Care

There are many things in life
That we cannot understand,
But we must trust God's judgment
And be guided by His hand,
And all who have God's blessing
Can rest safely in His Care
For He promises "safe passage"
On the "Wings of Faith and Prayer."

Part 2

Faith

There Is a Reason
for Everything

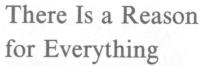

Our Father knows what's best for us,
So why should we complain—
We always want the sunshine,
But He knows there must be rain—
We love the sound of laughter
And the merriment of cheer,
But our hearts would lose their tenderness
If we never shed a tear . . .
Our Father tests us often
With suffering and with sorrow,
He tests us, not to punish us,
But to help us meet TOMORROW . . . *end*
For growing trees are strengthened
When they withstand the storm,

50

And the sharp cut of the chisel
Gives the marble grace and form . . .
God never hurts us needlessly,
And He never wastes our pain,
For every loss He sends to us
Is followed by rich gain . . .
And when we count the blessings
That God has so freely sent,
We will find no cause for murmuring
And no time to lament
For Our Father loves His children,
And to Him all things are plain,
So He never sends us PLEASURES
When the SOUL'S DEEP NEED IS PAIN . . .
So whenever we are troubled,
And when everything goes wrong,
It is just God working in us
To make OUR SPIRIT STRONG.

With Faith in Each Other
and Faith in the Lord

With Faith in Each Other
  and Faith in the Lord
May your Marriage be Blessed
  with love's priceless reward,
For love that endures
  and makes life worth living
Is built on strong Faith
  and unselfish giving . . .
So have Faith, and the Lord
  will guide Both of You through
The glorious New Life
  that is waiting for You.

. . . for with God all things are possible.

Mark 10:27

One of the Author's Favorite Prayers

GOD, open my eyes so I may see
And feel YOUR PRESENCE close to me . . .
Give me strength for my stumbling feet
As I battle the crowd on life's busy street,
And widen the vision of my unseeing eyes
So in passing faces I'll recognize
Not just a stranger, unloved and unknown,
But a friend with a heart that is much like my own . . .
Give me perception to make me aware
That scattered profusely on life's thoroughfare
Are the best GIFTS of GOD that we daily pass by
As we look at the world with an UNSEEING EYE.

There Is No Death

There is no night without a dawning,
No Winter without a Spring,
And beyond death's dark horizon
Our hearts once more will sing—
For those who leave us for a while
Have only GONE AWAY
Out of a restless, careworn world
Into a "BRIGHTER DAY"
Where there will be no partings
And time is not counted by years,
Where there are no trials or troubles,
No worries, no cares and no tears.

A Consolation Meditation

On the wings
  of death and sorrow
God sends us
  new hope for tomorrow—
And in His mercy
  and His grace
He gives us strength
  to bravely face
The lonely days
  that stretch ahead
And know our loved one
  is not dead
But only sleeping
  and out of our sight
And we'll meet in that land
  WHERE THERE IS NO NIGHT.

Death Is the Gateway to Eternal Life

Death is just another step along life's changing way,
No more than just a gateway
  to a new and better day,
And parting from our loved ones is much easier to bear
When we know that they are waiting
  for us to join them "There"—
For it is on the Wings of Death that the living soul takes flight
Into the "Promised Land of God"
  where there shall be "No Night"—
So death is just a natural thing,
  like the closing of a door,
As we start upon a journey
  to a new and distant shore—
And none need make this journey undirected or alone,
For God promised us safe passage
  to this vast and great unknown—
So let your grief be softened and yield not to despair,
You have only placed your loved one
  in the loving Father's care.

. . . Be not afraid, only believe.

Mark 5:36

A Teenager's Prayer

God, here I am in a "chaotic state"
Seeking some way to do "something great" . . .
I want to be someone who contributes to make
A less violent world for everyone's sake . . .
But who can I go to and who can I trust,
Who'll show me the difference between love and lust?
I'm willing to listen, I'm willing to do
Whatever it takes to make this world "new" . . .
But in the confusion and the noise all around
Where can the answer to my question be found?
Dear God up in heaven, hear a teenager's plea—
Show me somewhere what You want me to be!

"I Meet God
in the Morning"

"The earth is the Lord's
    and the fulness thereof"—
It speaks of His greatness,
    it sings of His love,
And each day at dawning
    I lift my heart high
And raise up my eyes
    to the infinite sky . . .
I watch the night vanish
    as a new day is born,
And I hear the birds sing
    on the wings of the morn,
I see the dew glisten
    in crystal-like splendor
While God, with a touch
    that is gentle and tender,
Wraps up the night
    and softly tucks it away
And hangs out the sun
    to herald a new day . . .
And so I give thanks
    and my heart kneels to pray—
"God keep me and guide me
    and go with me today.

**. . . all the earth shall be filled
with the glory of the Lord.**

Numbers 14:21

In God We Trust

O God, our Help in Ages Past,
  our Hope in Years To Be,
Look down upon this PRESENT
  and see our need of THEE—
For in this age of unrest,
  with danger all around,
We need Thy hand to lead us
  to higher, safer ground,
We need Thy help and counsel
  to make us more aware
That our safety and security
  lie solely in Thy care—
And as we FIGHT FOR FREEDOM
  make our way and purpose clear
And in our hours of danger
  may we feel Thy Presence near.

In God's Tomorrow There Is Eternal Spring

All nature heeds the call of Spring
As GOD awakens everything,
And all that seemed so dead and still
Experiences a sudden thrill
As Springtime lays a magic hand
Across GOD'S vast and fertile land—
Oh, how can anyone stand by
And watch a sapphire Springtime sky
Or see a fragile flower break through
What just a day ago or two
Seemed barren ground still hard with frost,
But in GOD'S world no life is lost,
And flowers sleep beneath the ground
But when they hear Spring's waking sound
They push themselves through layers of clay
To reach the sunlight of GOD'S DAY—
And man, like flowers, too, must sleep
Until he is called from the "darkened deep"
To live in that place where angels sing
And where there is ETERNAL SPRING!

Life's Bitterest Disappointments Are God's Sweetest Appointments

Out of life's misery born of man's sins
A fuller, richer life begins,
For when we are helpless with no place to go
And our hearts are heavy and our spirits are low,
If we place our poor, broken lives in GOD'S HANDS
And surrender completely to HIS WILL and DEMANDS,
The "darkness lifts" and the "sun shines through"
And by HIS TOUCH we are "born anew" . . .
So praise GOD for trouble that "cuts like a knife"
And disappointments that shatter your life,
For with PATIENCE to WAIT and FAITH to ENDURE
Your life will be blessed and your future secure,
For GOD is but testing your FAITH and your LOVE
Before HE "APPOINTS YOU" to rise far above
All the small things that so sorely distress you,
For GOD'S only intention is to strengthen and bless you.

Wherefore let them that suffer according to the will of God commit the keeping of their souls to him in well doing, as unto a faithful Creator.

1 Peter 4:19

Live by Faith and Not by Feelings

When everything is pleasant and bright
And the things we do turn out just right,
We feel without question that GOD is real,
For, when we are happy, how good we feel . . .
But when the tides turn and gone is the song
And misfortune comes and our plans go wrong,
Doubt creeps in and we start to wonder
And our thoughts about GOD are torn asunder—
For we feel deserted in time of deep stress,
Without GOD'S PRESENCE to assure us and bless . . .
And it is then when our senses are reeling
We realize clearly it's FAITH and not FEELING—
For it takes GREAT FAITH to patiently wait,
Believing "GOD comes NOT TOO SOON or TOO LATE."

All Nature
Tells Us Nothing
Really Ever Dies

Nothing really ever dies
That is not born anew—
The MIRACLES of NATURE
All tell us this is true . . .
The flowers sleeping peacefully
Beneath the Winter's snow
Awaken from their icy grave
When Spring winds start to blow
And little brooks and singing streams,
Icebound beneath the snow,
Begin to babble merrily
Beneath the sun's warm glow . . .
And all around on every side
New life and joy appear
To tell us NOTHING EVER DIES
And we should have no fear,
For death is just a detour
Along life's wending way
That leads GOD'S chosen children
To a bright and glorious day.

The Promises of Man
May Fail but
God's Promises Prevail

In this uncertain world of trouble
With its sorrow, sin and strife
Man needs a haven for his heart
To endure the "storms of life" . . .
He keeps hoping for a promise
Of better, bigger things
With the power and the prestige
That fame and fortune brings . . .
And the world is rife with promises
That are fast and falsely spoken
For man in his deceptive way

Knows his promise can be broken . . .
But when GOD makes a promise
It remains forever true
For everything GOD promises
He unalterably will do . . .
So read the promises of GOD
That will never fail or falter
And inherit EVERLASTING LIFE
Which even death can't alter . . .
And when you're disillusioned
And every hope is blighted
Recall the promises of GOD
And your FAITH will be relighted,
Knowing there's ONE LASTING PROMISE
On which man can depend,
And that's the PROMISE of SALVATION
And a LIFE THAT HAS NO END.

God Is the Answer

We read the headlines daily
and we listen to the news,
We are anxious and bewildered
with the world's conflicting views,
We are restless and dissatisfied
and sadly insecure,
And we voice our discontentment
over things we must endure,
For this violent age we live in
is filled with nameless fears
That grow as we discuss the things
that come daily to our ears . . .
So, instead of reading headlines
that disturb the heart and mind,
Let us open up the Bible
and in doing so we'll find
That this age is no different
from the millions gone before,
But in every hour of crisis
God has opened up a door
For all who sought His guidance
and trusted in His plan,
For God provides the Answer
that cannot be found by man . . .
And though there's hate and violence
and dissension all around,
We can always find a refuge
that is built on "solid ground"
If we go to God believing
that He hears our smallest prayer
And that nothing can befall us
when we are in His care . . .

For only by believing
in the things We Cannot See
Can All Nations Be United
in the Peace that makes Men Free . . .
For the skill of man can conquer
new worlds in outer space,
But only our Creator
can endow mankind with grace,
And only grace that is divine
can unite us with each other
And make our enemies our friends
and Every Man A Brother.

Life Is Eternal

"LIFE IS ETERNAL," the GOOD LORD said,
So do not think of your loved one as dead—
For death is only a stepping stone
To a beautiful life we have never known,
A place where GOD promised man he would be
Eternally happy and safe and free,
A wonderful land where we live anew
When our journey on earth is over and through—
So trust in GOD and doubt HIM never
For all who love HIM live forever,
And while we cannot understand
Just let the SAVIOUR take your hand,
For when DEATH'S ANGEL comes to call
"GOD is so GREAT and we're so small" . . .
And there is nothing you need fear
For FAITH IN GOD makes all things clear.

His soul shall dwell at ease . . .

Psalms 25:13

Faith Is a Candle

In this sick world of hatred
And violence and sin,
Where men renounce morals
And reject discipline,
We stumble in "darkness"
Groping vainly for "light"
To distinguish the difference
Between Wrong and Right,
But Dawn cannot follow
This Night of Despair
Unless Faith Lights a Candle
In All Hearts Everywhere
And warmed by the glow
Our hate melts away
And Love Lights the Path
To a Peaceful, New Day.

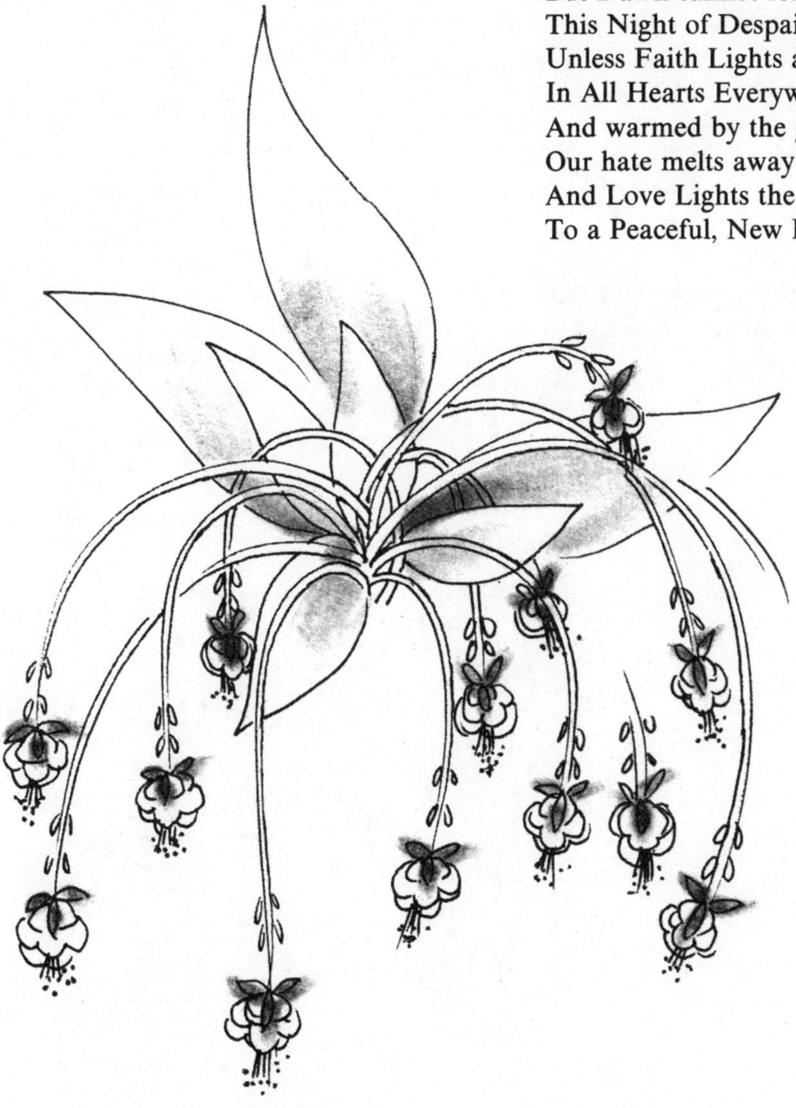

Never Be Discouraged

There is really nothing we need know
　　or even try to understand
If we refuse to be discouraged
　　and trust God's Guiding Hand . . .
So take heart and meet each minute
　　with Faith in God's Great Love,
Aware that every day of life
　　is controlled by God Above . . .
And never dread Tomorrow
　　or what the Future brings,
Just pray for strength and courage
　　and trust God in all things . . .
And never grow discouraged
　　be patient and just wait
For "God never comes too early
　　and He Never Comes Too Late!"

**Cast thy burden upon the Lord,
and he shall sustain thee . . .**

Psalms 55:22

A Tribute to
the Patron Saint of Love

*opening
Jan 4 - 2000*

Where there is love the heart is light,
Where there is love the day is bright,
Where there is love there is a song
To help when things are going wrong,
Where there is love there is a smile
To make all things seem more worthwhile,
Where there is love there's quiet peace,
A tranquil place where turmoils cease—
Love changes darkness into light
And makes the heart take "wingless flight"—
Oh, blest are they who walk in love,
They also walk with God above—
For God is love and through love alone
Man finds the joy that the SAINTS have known.

Who Said, "God Is Dead"?

In this world of new concepts
   it has often been said—
Why heed the Commandments
   of a God who is dead.
Why follow His precepts
   that are old and outdated,
Restrictive and narrow
   and in no way related
To this modern-day world
   where the pace is so fast
It cannot be hampered
   by an old-fashioned past . . .
And yet this "DEAD GOD"
   still holds in His Hand
The star-studded sky,
   the sea and the land.

And with perfect precision
    the old earth keeps spinning
As flawlessly accurate
    as in "THE BEGINNING" . . .
So be not deceived
    by "the new pharisees"
Who boast man has only
    HIS OWN SELF TO PLEASE,
And who loudly proclaim
    any man is a fool
Who denies himself pleasure
    to follow God's rule . . .
But what can they offer
    that will last and endure
And make life's uncertainties
    safe and secure,
And what, though man gain
    the whole world and its pleasures,
If he loses his soul
    and "eternity's treasures"?

We Can't Have a "Crown"
Without a "Cross"

We all have those days
  that are dismal and dreary
And we feel sorta blue
  and lonely and weary,
But we have to admit
  that life is worth living
And GOD gives us reasons
  for daily "THANKSGIVING" . . .
For life's an experience
  GOD'S CHILDREN go through
That's made up of gladness
  and much sadness, too . . .
But we have to know both
  the "BITTER" and "SWEET"
If we want a GOOD LIFE
  that is FULL and COMPLETE,
For each trial we suffer
  and every shed tear
Just gives us NEW STRENGTH
  to PERSEVERE.

This Is My Prayer

Bless us, heavenly Father,
  Forgive our erring ways,
Grant us strength to serve Thee,
  Put purpose in our days . . .
Give us understanding
  Enough to make us kind
So we may judge all people
  With our heart and not our mind . . .
And teach us to be patient
  In everything we do,
Content to trust Your wisdom
  And to follow after You . . .
And help us when we falter
  And hear us when we pray
And receive us in THY KINGDOM
  To dwell with Thee some day.

This is my prayer that I faithfully say
  To help me to meet the new dawning day,
For I never could meet life's daily demands
  Unless I was sure He was holding my hands . . .
And priceless indeed would be my reward
  To know that you shared My Prayer To the Lord.

"Trust" Is a "Must"

"I have no FAITH," the skeptic cries,
"I can only accept what I see with my eyes" ...
Yet man has to have FAITH or he would never complete
Just a simple task like crossing the street,
For he has to have FAITH in his manly stride
To get him across to the other side,
And the world would be panic-stricken indeed
If no one thought that he could succeed
In doing the smallest, simplest thing
That life with its many demands can bring ...
So why do the skeptics still ridicule
And call "THE MAN of FAITH" a fool
When FAITH is the BASIS of all that we do—
And that includes UNBELIEVERS, too.

Today, Tomorrow,
and Always He Is There

In sickness or health,
In suffering and pain,
In storm-laden skies,
In sunshine and rain,
GOD ALWAYS IS THERE
To lighten your way
And lead you through "darkness"
To a much brighter day.

. . . the Lord will hear when I call unto him.

Psalms 4:3

Today's Joy Was Born of
Yesterday's Sorrow

Who said the "darkness of the night"
  would never turn to day,
Who said the "winter's bleakness"
  would never pass away,
Who said the fog would never lift
  and let the sunshine through,
Who said the skies now overcast
  would nevermore be blue—
Why should we ever entertain
  these thoughts so dark and grim
And let the brightness of our mind
  grow cynical and dim
When we know beyond all questioning
  that winter turns to spring
And on the notes of sorrow
  new songs are made to sing—
For no one sheds a teardrop
  or suffers loss in vain,
For God is always there to turn
  our losses into gain,
And every burden born TODAY
  and every present sorrow
Are but God's happy harbingers
  of a joyous, bright TOMORROW.

"Thy Will Be Done"

God did not promise "sun without rain,"
   "light without darkness" or "joy without pain"—
He only promised us "STRENGTH for the DAY"
   when "the darkness" comes and we lose our way,
For only through sorrow do we grow more aware
   that God is our refuge in times of despair . . .
For when we are happy and life's bright and fair,
   we often forget to kneel down in prayer,
But God seems much closer and needed much more
   when trouble and sorrow stand outside our door—
For then we seek shelter in His wondrous love
   and we ask Him to send us help from above . . .
And that is the reason we know it is true
   that bright, shining hours and dark, sad ones, too,
Are part of the plan God made for each one,
   and all we can pray is "THY WILL BE DONE"!

A Child's Prayer

Hear me, Blessed Jesus
  as I say my prayers today
And tell me you are close to me,
  and you'll never go away,
And tell me that you love me
  like the Bible says you do,
And tell me also, Jesus,
  I can always come to you
And you will understand me
  when other people don't,
And though some may forget me
  just tell me that you won't—
And, Jesus, stay real close to me
  at home and school and play,
For I will feel much braver
  if you're never far away—
And sometimes when I'm naughty,
  I hope you won't be sad,

For really I don't mean to do
   anything that's bad—
And most of all, dear Jesus,
   it's your birthday and I know
Out Father sent you to us
   to live on earth below
So little children like myself
   would know you too were small,
And that you are our dearest friend
   and you understand us all—
And, Jesus, I like Christmas
   for the presents that it brings,
But I know YOUR LOVE is GREATER
   than all the other things—
And some day when I'm older
   I will show you it is true
That even as a little child
   MY HEART BELONGED TO YOU.

Be ye therefore followers of God, as dear children.

Ephesians 5:1

This Is Just a Resting Place

Sometimes the road of life seems long
   as we travel through the years
And, with a heart that's broken
   and eyes brimful of tears,
We falter in our weariness
   and sink beside the way,
But GOD leans down and whispers,
   "Child, there'll be another day"—
And the road will grow much smoother
   and much easier to face,
So do not be disheartened—
   this is just a "RESTING PLACE."

Faith Is the Key
to Heaven

Oh, FATHER, grant once more to men
A SIMPLE, CHILDLIKE FAITH again,
Forgetting COLOR, RACE, and CREED
And seeing only the heart's deep
   need . . .
For FAITH alone can save man's soul
And lead him to a HIGHER GOAL,
For there's but one unfailing course—
We win by FAITH and NOT by FORCE.

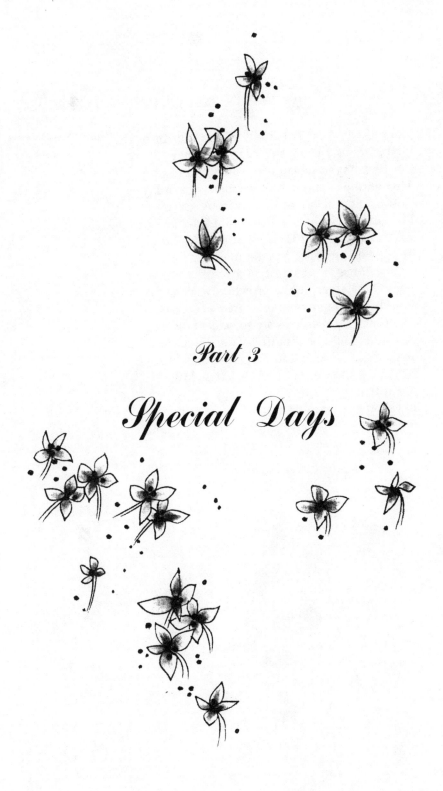

Part 3

Special Days

A New Year! A New Day! A New Life!

Not only on *New Year's* but all the year through
God gives us a chance to begin life anew,
For each day at dawning we have but to pray
That all the mistakes that we made yesterday
Will be blotted out and forgiven by grace,
For God in His love will completely efface
All that is past and He'll grant a new start
To all who are truly repentant at heart—
And well may man pause in awesome-like wonder
That Our Father in heaven who dwells far asunder
Could still remain willing to freely forgive
The shabby, small lives we so selfishly live
And still would be mindful of sin-ridden man
Who constantly goes on defying God's Plan—
But this is the *Gift* of God's limitless love
A gift that we all are so unworthy of,
But God gave it to us and all we need do
Is to ask God's forgiveness and begin life anew.

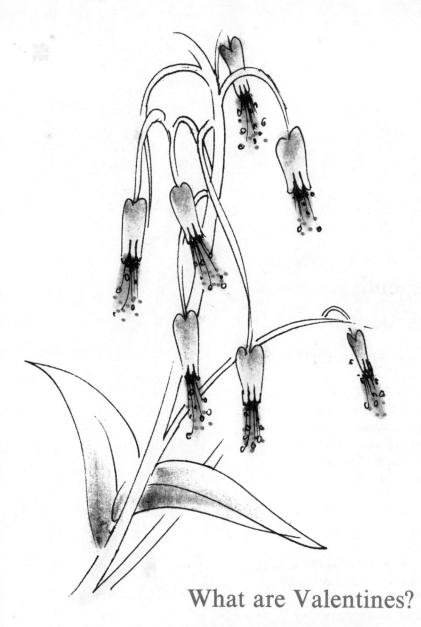

What are Valentines?

Valentines are GIFTS of LOVE
And with the help of God above
Love can change the human race
And make this world a better place—
For love dissolves all hate and fear
And makes our vision bright and clear
So we can see and rise above
Our pettiness on "wings of love."

Be kindly affectioned one to another . . .

Romans 12:10

The Legend
of the Valentine

The legend says ST. VALENTINE
Was in a prison cell
Thinking of his little flock
He had always loved so well
And, wanting to assure them
Of his friendship and his love,
He picked a bunch of violets
And sent them by a dove . . .

And on the violets' velvet leaves
He pierced these lines divine
That simply said, "I LOVE YOU"
And "I'M YOUR VALENTINE" . . .
So through the years that followed,
From that day unto this,
Folks still send messages of love
And seal them with a kiss . . .

Because a SAINT in prison
Reached through prison bars one day
And picked a bunch of violets
And sent them out to say
That FAITH and LOVE can triumph,
No matter where you are,
For FAITH and LOVE are GREATER
Than the strongest prison bar.

Springtime Glory

Flowers buried
beneath the snow
Awakening again to live and grow—
Leaves that fell to the earth to die
Enriching the soil in which they lie—
Lifeless-looking, stark,
stripped trees
Bursting with buds
in the Springtime breeze
Are just a few examples of
The greatness of God's power and love,
And in this blaze of Springtime glory
Just who could doubt
the Easter Story!

An Easter Prayer for Peace

Our Father, up in heaven,
  hear this Easter prayer:
May the people of ALL NATIONS
  BE UNITED IN THY CARE,
For earth's peace and man's salvation
  can come only by Thy grace
And not through bombs and missiles
  and our quest for outer space . . .
For until all men recognize
  that "THE BATTLE IS THE LORD'S"
And peace on earth can not be won
  with strategy and swords,
We will go on vainly fighting,
  as we have in ages past,
Finding only empty victories
  and a peace that cannot last . . .
But we've grown so rich and mighty
  and so arrogantly strong,
We no longer ask in humbleness—
  "God, show us where we're wrong" . . .

We have come to trust completely
 in the power of man-made things,
Unmindful of God's mighty power
 and that HE IS "KING OF KINGS" . . .
We have turned our eyes from HIM
 to go our selfish way,
And money, power, and pleasure
 are the gods we serve today . . .
And the good green earth God gave us
 to peacefully enjoy,
Through greed and fear and hatred
 we are seeking to destroy . . .
Oh, Father, up in heaven,
 stir and wake our sleeping souls,
Renew our faith and lift us up
 and give us higher goals,
And grant us heavenly guidance
 as Easter comes again—
For, more than GUIDED MISSILES,
 all the world needs GUIDED MEN.

The Lord is good, a strong hold in the day
of trouble; and he knoweth them that trust in him.

Nahum 1:7

91

The Promise of Easter
"Because He Lives
We Too Shall Live"

We need these seven words above
  to help us to endure
The changing world around us
  that is dark and insecure,
To help us view the present
  as a passing episode,
A troubled, brief encounter
  on life's short and troubled road—
For in knowing life's eternal
  because our Saviour died
And arose again at Easter
  after He was crucified
Makes this uncertain present,
  in a world of sin and strife,
Nothing but a stepping-stone
  to a NEW and BETTER LIFE!

An Easter Promise

If we but had the eyes to see
God's face in every cloud,
If we but had the ears to hear
His voice above the crowd
If we could feel His gentle touch
In every Springtime breeze
And find a haven in His arms
"Neath sheltering, leafy trees . . .
If we could just lift up our hearts
Like flowers to the sun
And trust His *Easter Promise*
And Pray, *"Thy Will Be Done"*,
We'd find the peace we're seeking,
The kind no man can give,
The peace that comes from knowing
He Died So We Might Live!

**For God so loved the world,
that he gave his only begotten Son,
that whosoever believeth in him
should not perish, but have everlasting life.**

John 3:16

The Miracles of Easter

The sleeping earth awakens,
The robins start to sing,
The flowers open wide their eyes
To tell us it is Spring,
The bleakness of the Winter
Is melted by the sun,
The tree that looked so stark and dead
Becomes a living one . . .
These MIRACLES of EASTER,
Wrought with divine perfection,
Are the blessed reassurance
Of our Saviour's Resurrection.

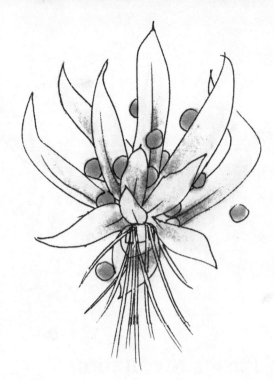

Easter Thoughts for These Troubled Times

As the Easter Season
  dawns once again,
We look on a world
  of restless men—
Men who are "driven"
  by fear and greed
And caught in a web
  of tension and speed,
Driving themselves
  and the world, as well,
Into a future
  no one can foretell—
Oh, God, instead
  of vain "driven men,"
Fill man's heart
  with true "DRIVE" again,
Spurred on by FAITH
  in GOD ABOVE
To build a new world
  of "BROTHERLY LOVE."

An Easter Meditation

In the glorious Easter Story
A troubled world can find
Blessed reassurance
And enduring peace of mind—
For though we grow discouraged
In this world we're living in,
There is comfort just in knowing
That God triumphed over sin,
For our Saviour's Resurrection
Was God's way of telling men
That in Christ we are eternal
And in Him we live again—
And to know life is unending
And God's love is endless, too,
Makes our daily tasks and burdens
So much easier to do,
And our earthly trials and problems
Are but guideposts on the way
To the love and life eternal
That God promised Easter Day.

**. . . [Jesus Christ] hath abolished death,
and hath brought life and immortality
to light through the gospel.**

2 Timothy 1:10

Rejoice! Rejoice!

"Let Not Your Heart Be Troubled"—
Let not your soul be sad—
Easter is a time of joy
When all hearts should be glad,
Glad to know that Jesus Christ
Made it possible for men
To have their sins forgiven
And, like Him, to live again . . .
So at this joyous season
May the wondrous Easter Story
Renew our Faith so we may be
Partakers of "His Glory!"

A Mother's Day Prayer

"OUR FATHER in HEAVEN
  whose love is divine,
Thanks for the love
  of a Mother like mine—
And in Thy great mercy
  look down from Above
And grant this dear Mother
  the GIFT of YOUR LOVE—
And all through the year,
  whatever betide her,
Assure her each day
  that You are beside her—
And, Father in Heaven,
  show me the way
To lighten her tasks
  and brighten her day,
And bless her dear heart
  with the insight to see
That her love means more
  than the world to me."

Her children arise up, and call her blessed . . .

Proverbs 31:28

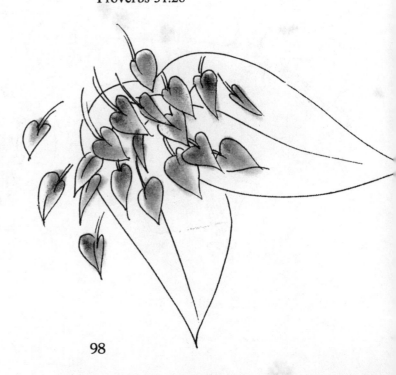

Mother's Day

MOTHER'S DAY IS REMEMBRANCE DAY
And we pause on The Path Of The Year
To pay honor and worshipful tribute
To the Mother our heart holds dear . . .
For, whether here or in heaven,
Her love is our haven and guide.
For always the memory of Mother
Is a beacon light shining inside . . .
Time cannot destroy her memory
And years can never erase
The tenderness and the beauty
Of the love in a Mother's face . . .
And, when we think of our Mother,
We draw nearer to God above,
For only God in His Greatness
Could fashion a MOTHER'S LOVE.

It's So Nice to Have a Dad Around the House

DADS are special people
No home should be without,
For every family will agree
They're "SO NICE TO HAVE ABOUT"—
They are a happy mixture
Of a "SMALL BOY" and a "MAN"
And they're very necessary
In every "FAMILY PLAN"—
Sometimes they're most demanding
And stern, and firm and tough,
But underneath they're "soft as silk"
For this is just a "BLUFF"—
But in any kind of trouble
Dad reaches out his hand,
And you can always count on him
To help and understand—
And while we do not praise Dad
As often as we should,
We love him and admire him,
And while that's understood,
It's only fair to emphasize
His importance and his worth—
For if there were no loving Dads
This would be a "LOVELESS EARTH!"

Best Wishes to a "Model" Dad on Father's Day

Father's Day is one of those days
When Dads like you deserve some praise,
And this is coming just to say
You're wished a happy Father's Day,
And you're so dear and thoughtful, too,
More Dads should be "modeled" after you.

A Prayer for the Bride

Oh, God of love look down and bless
This radiant bride with happiness,
And fill her heart with "Love's Sweet Song"
Enough to last her whole life long—
And give her patience when things disturb
So she can somehow gently curb
Hasty words in anger spoken,
Leaving two hearts sad and broken—
And give her guidance all through life
And keep her a loving, faithful wife.

A Prayer for
the Bride and Groom

As hand in hand you enter
  a life that's bright and new,
May God look down from heaven
  and bless the two of you;
May He give you understanding
  enough to make you kind,
So you may judge each other
  with your heart and not your mind;
May He teach you to be patient
  as you learn to live together,
Forgiving little "human rifts"
  that arise in "stormy weather"—
And may your love be big enough
  to withstand the strongest sea
So you may dwell forever
  in love's rich tranquility.

Two are better than one . . .

Ecclesiastes 4:9

For the New Bride

And now you are *Mrs.* instead of *Miss,*
And you've sealed your wedding vows
with a kiss,
Your Future lies in *Your Hands,* my dear,
For it's yours to mold
from year to year . . .
God grant that you make it
a beautiful thing
With all of the blessings that marriage
can bring,
May you and the fine, lucky man
of your choice
Find daily new blessings to make you rejoice,
And year after year may you go on together
Always finding a "rainbow"
regardless of weather . . .
And when youthful charms have faded away
May you look back with joy to your
glad *Wedding Day*
And thank God for helping
to make you a *Wife*
Who discovered the blessings of a
full married life.

Congratulations

Your marriage has been truly blessed
For with your new son's birth,
God sent an Angel down from Heaven
To live with you on earth
For I think God UP IN HEAVEN
Looks down on couples in love
And blesses their happy union
With a Gift of His Love FROM ABOVE . . .
And so through this Tiny Angel
He has drawn you together for life,
For now you are Father and Mother
Instead of just husband and wife . . .
And while he is yours to fondle,
To care for, to teach, and to love,
He belongs to His Father IN HEAVEN,
For he came from His Home UP ABOVE . . .
So ask Him for guidance in molding
The future of your little boy,
For he is a "Jewel" from His Kingdom
Sent to bring you Heavenly Joy!

**Thy father and thy mother shall be glad,
and she that bare thee shall rejoice.**

Proverbs 23:25

For a Young Person at Confirmation

When we are confirmed
   in the FAITH of THE LORD,
Our greatest possession
   and richest reward
Is knowing that now
   we are HERALDS of THE KING,
Ready His praises
   and glory to sing—
And, oh, what a privilege
   to witness for God
And to walk in the way
   that the dear Saviour trod,
Confirmed in THE FAITH
   and upheld by HIS HAND,
Eager to follow
   His smallest command—
Secure in the knowledge
   that though now and then
We're guilty of sins
   that are common to men,

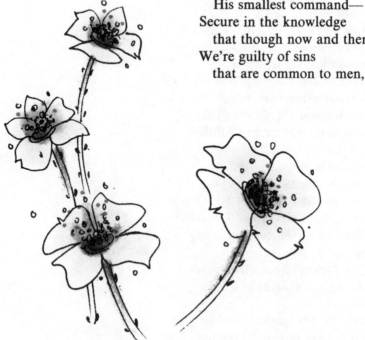

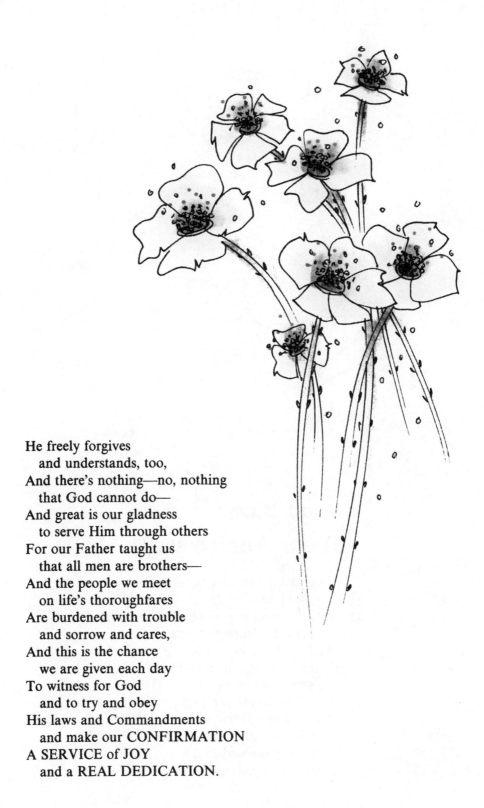

He freely forgives
   and understands, too,
And there's nothing—no, nothing
   that God cannot do—
And great is our gladness
   to serve Him through others
For our Father taught us
   that all men are brothers—
And the people we meet
   on life's thoroughfares
Are burdened with trouble
   and sorrow and cares,
And this is the chance
   we are given each day
To witness for God
   and to try and obey
His laws and Commandments
   and make our CONFIRMATION
A SERVICE of JOY
   and a REAL DEDICATION.

God Bless
Your Anniversary

This happy anniversary proves
  a fact you can't disparage—
It takes true Love and Faith and Hope
  to make a Happy Marriage . . .
And it takes a lot of praying
  and a devoted man and wife
To keep God ever-present
  in their Home and in their Life . . .
And you're a grand example
  and an Inspiration, too,
And every married couple
  should be patterned after you.

An Anniversary Wish

As you recall that happy day
   that united you in love,
May you read this book together
   as The Lord smiles from above
And blesses you especially
   because through Faith and Prayer
You Took Him for a Partner
   and placed Your Marriage in His Care,
For it was by Divine Design
   that you two met each other
And then God made you "Man and Wife"
   and a loving Dad and Mother!

An Anniversary
Is Another Link of Love
Binding Couples Closer

It takes a special day like this
To just look back and reminisce
And think of all the things you've shared
Since the first day you knew "You Cared" . . .
Of course things Change for that is life
And love between a man and wife
Cannot remain "romantic bliss"
Forever "flavored with a kiss,"
But Always There's That Bond Of Love
There's Just No Explanation Of,
And with the "storms" and "trials" it grows
Like flowers do beneath the snows . . .
Sometimes it's hidden from the sight
Just like the sun gets lost in night,
But Always There's That Bond Of Love
There's Just No Explanation Of . . .
And Every Year That You're Together,
Regardless of the "kind of weather"—
The Bond Of Love Grows That Much Stronger
Because You've Shared It One Year Longer.

If we love one another, God dwelleth in us . . .

1 John 4:12

Another Anniversary!
Another Link of Love!

It only seems like yesterday
That you were a radiant bride
With a proud and happy bridegroom
Standing at your side—
And looking back across the years
On a happy day like this
Brings many treasured memories
As you fondly reminisce—
And while you've had your arguments
And little "tiffs," it's true,
And countless little problems
To vex and worry you,
For every "hurt and heartache"
And perhaps at times some "tears"
You've shared a world of happiness
Throughout your married years—
And looking back on this glad day
You both realize anew
That the sweetest words you ever said
Were just the words, "I Do"!

111

A Birthday Message
for Someone Who
Will Always Be Young

Some folks grow older with birthdays, it's true,
But others grow nicer as years widen their view,
And a heart that is young lends an aura of grace
That rivals in beauty a young, pretty face—
For no one would notice a few little wrinkles
When a kind, loving heart fills the eyes full of twinkles—
So don't count your years by the birthdays you've had,
But by things you have done to make Other Folks Glad!

Just for You
on Your Birthday

There are some that we meet in passing
And forget them as soon as they go—
There are some we remember with pleasure
And feel honored and privileged to know—
And You are that kind of a person
Who leaves lovely memories behind,
And special days like your Birthday
Bring many fond memories to mind—
And memories are priceless possessions
That time can never destroy
For it is in happy remembrance
The heart finds its greatest joy.

"One Nation Under God"

Thanksgiving is more
  than a day in November
That students of history
  are taught to remember,
More than a date
  that we still celebrate
With turkey and dressing
  piled high on our plate . . .
For while we still offer
  the traditional prayer,
We pray out of habit
  without being aware
That the pilgrims thanked God
  just for being alive,
For the strength that He gave them
  to endure and survive
Hunger and hardship
  that's unknown in the present
Where progress and plenty
  have made our lives pleasant . . .
And living today
  in this great and rich nation
that depends not on God
  but on mechanization,

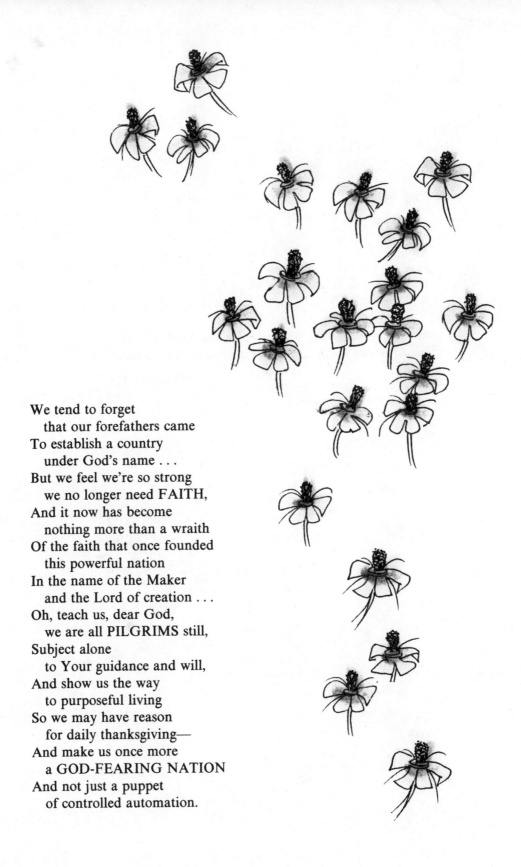

We tend to forget
   that our forefathers came
To establish a country
   under God's name . . .
But we feel we're so strong
   we no longer need FAITH,
And it now has become
   nothing more than a wraith
Of the faith that once founded
   this powerful nation
In the name of the Maker
   and the Lord of creation . . .
Oh, teach us, dear God,
   we are all PILGRIMS still,
Subject alone
   to Your guidance and will,
And show us the way
   to purposeful living
So we may have reason
   for daily thanksgiving—
And make us once more
   a GOD-FEARING NATION
And not just a puppet
   of controlled automation.

A Thanksgiving Day Prayer

"Faith of our Fathers" renew us again
And make us a nation of God-fearing men
Seeking Thy guidance, Thy love and Thy will,
For we are but Pilgrims in need of Thee still—
And, gathered together on Thanksgiving Day,
May we lift up our hearts and our hands as we pray
To thank You for blessings we so little merit
And grant us Thy love and teach us to SHARE IT.

**Blessed is the nation whose God is the Lord; and the
people whom he hath chosen for his own inheritance.**

Psalms 33:12

A Christmas Meditation

Give us through the coming year
QUIETNESS of MIND,
Teach us to be PATIENT
And always to be KIND,
Give us REASSURANCE
When everything goes wrong
So our FAITH remains unfaltering
And our HOPE and COURAGE strong—
And show us that in QUIETNESS
We can feel Your Presence near
Filling us with JOY and PEACE
Throughout the coming year.

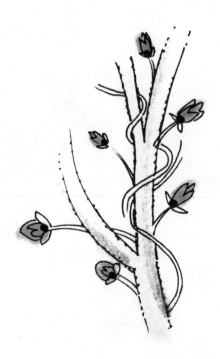

A Christmas Thought

If there had never been a Christmas
  or the Holy Christ Child's birth,
Or the angels singing in the sky
  of promised PEACE on EARTH—
What would the world be like today
  with no ETERNAL GOAL,
What would the temporal body be
  without a living soul—
Just what would give us courage
  to push on when hope is dead
Except the Christmas message
  and the words OUR FATHER said—
"In love I send My only Son
  to live and die for you,
And through His resurrection
  you will gain a new life, too."

Christmastime
Is Friendship Time

At Christmastime our hearts reach out
To friends we think of dearly
And checking through our Friendship lists,
As all of us do yearly,
We stop a while to reminisce
And to pleasantly review
Happy little happenings
And things we used to do—
And though we've been too busy
To keep in touch all year,
We send a Christmas greeting
At this season of GOOD CHEER—
So Christmas is a "lovely link"
Between old years and new
That keeps the "Bond of Friendship"
Forever unbroken and true.

. . . a little child shall lead them.

Isaiah 11:6

"The Story of the Infant of Prague"

The Gentle Little Jesus Child came as a Gift of Love
From Our Father up in Heaven with a message from above . . .
His birth was in a stable in Bethlehem, we know,
But an Image of The Infant many centuries ago
Was given to The Carmelites by a Princess who was good,
And in Prague upon an altar this Holy Infant stood . . .
And many came to worship for the kindly Princess said:
"This is the Saviour of mankind," and so the story spread
Of how the Holy Infant brought comfort, peace and light
And victory to Prague's army as it battled for the right—
For according to the story in the centuries gone by,
A King invoked The Infant for help from God on high,
And many other miracles have divinely taken place
When men knelt before the altar and invoked The Infant's Grace . . .

For Jesus is The Father's Son who was sent to earth below
So mankind might feel God's Presence and better come to know
The nearness of the Father through His beloved Son,
And as the gentle Jesus prayed, "Father, Thy Will be Done,"
He purchased our salvation with His blood upon the cross,
And if we believe in Jesus we can never suffer loss . . .
And the more you honor Jesus, the more the Lord will bless
Your life with truth and virtue and faith and happiness . . .
And this great Gift of God's dear love is within the reach of all
Through Mary's intercession and the Infant Child so small,
For Jesus said: "Come Unto Me And I Will Give You Rest"
For My Father up in heaven knows all your troubles best—
And Jesus told the multitude, "Ask And You Shall Receive"
For anything is possible if you trust Him and believe . . .
And in praying to The Infant for guidance from above
We come closer to Our Father And His Great Unfailing Love.

He's the Saviour of the World

All the world has heard the story
  of the LITTLE CHRIST CHILD'S BIRTH,
But too few have felt the meaning
  of His mission here on earth . . .
Some regard it as a story
  that is beautiful to hear,
A lovely Christmas custom
  that we celebrate each year . . .
But it is more than just a story
  told to make our hearts rejoice,
It's OUR FATHER up in heaven
  speaking through the Christ Child's voice,
Telling us of heavenly kingdoms
  that He has prepared above
For all who trust His mercy
  and live only for His love . . .
And only through the Christ Child
  can man be born again,
For God sent the BABY JESUS
  as the SAVIOUR OF ALL MEN.

Let Us Bring Him
a Gift of Joy as Did
the Little Drummer Boy

As once more we approach
  the Birthday of OUR KING—
Do we search our hearts
  for a GIFT we can bring,
Do we stand by in awe
  like the small DRUMMER BOY
Who had no rare jewels,
  not even a toy,
To lay at Christ's Crib
  like the Wise Men of old
Who brought precious gifts
  of Silver and Gold—
But the Drummer Boy played
  for the Infant Child
And the Baby Jesus
  looked up and smiled,
For the boy had given
  the best that he had
And his gift from the heart
  made the Saviour glad—
And today He still smiles
  on all those who bring
THEIR HEARTS to lay
  at the FEET OF THE KING.

Rejoice! It's Christmas!

May the holy remembrance
   of the FIRST CHRISTMAS DAY
Be our reassurance
   CHRIST is not far away . . .
For on Christmas HE came
   to walk here on earth,
So let us find joy
   in the news of HIS birth . . .

And let us find comfort
   and strength for each day
In knowing that Christ
   walked this same earthly way . . .
So He knows all our needs
   and He hears every prayer
And He keeps all "His children"
   always safe in His care . . .
And whenever we're troubled
   and lost in despair
We have but to seek Him
   and ask Him in prayer
To guide and direct us
   and help us to bear
Our sickness and sorrow,
   our worry and care . . .
So once more at Christmas
   let the whole world rejoice
In the knowledge He answers
   every prayer that we voice.

In Christ Who Was Born At Christmas
All Men May Live Again

Let us all remember
When our faith is running low,
Christ is more than just a figure
Wrapped in an ethereal glow—
For He came and dwelt among us
And He knows our every need
And He loves and understands us
And forgives each sinful deed—
He was crucified and buried
And rose again in glory
And His promise of salvation
Makes the wondrous Christmas Story
An abiding reassurance
That the little Christ Child's birth
Was the beautiful beginning
Of God's Plan for PEACE on EARTH.

Mother Is the Heart of the Home and the Home Is the Heart of Christmas

Memories to treasure are made of Christmas Day,
Made of family gatherings and children as they play . . .

And always it is MOTHER who plays the leading part
In bringing joy and happiness to each expectant heart . . .

These memories grow more meaningful with every passing year,
More precious and more beautiful, more treasured and more dear . . .

And that is why at Christmastime there comes the happy thought
Of all these treasured memories that Mother's love has brought . . .

For no one gives more happiness or does more good for others
Than understanding, kind and wise and selfless, loving Mothers . . .

And of all the loving Mothers, the dearest one is YOU,
For you live Christmas EVERY DAY in EVERY THING YOU DO!

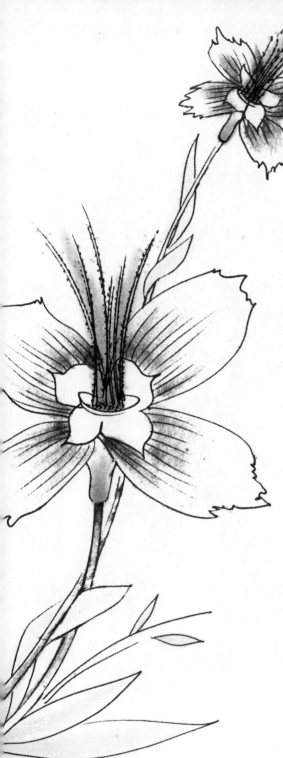

With His Love

If you found any beauty
   in the poems in this book
Or some peace and comfort
   in a word or a line,
Don't give me the praise
   or worldly acclaim
For the words that you read
   are not mine . . .
I borrowed them all
   to share with you
From our
   HEAVENLY FATHER ABOVE.
And the joy that you felt
   Was God speaking to you
  As HE flooded your heart
   with HIS LOVE.

**Thy word is a lamp unto my feet,
and a light unto my path.**

Psalms 119:105